To Melanie who
encouraged me to write
something new every day
and who read the best and
the worst of everything
I've written, and to James
who told me to go for it
and everyone else who has
inspired and helped me.
But mainly to Liam, who is
the reason I swapped to a
pen to start with.

Thank you.

Throw your watercolours
into the ocean.

Know hope.

ISBN: 978-1-4717-9236-
6

Contents

Begin At The Sea

Dangling my legs over the
edge of the cool, damp,
rough rock
Bare toes dipped
precautiously into the
bitter, salty water
Waves lapping at the sand
Crashing at the rocks,
around my ankles
The salty sea air batters
about me
Leaving a fresh fragrance
in my hair, as it whips
about my cold, damp face.

I wish I could bottle up the
sea breeze
And take it wherever I
went
A piece of home

Trapped within glass.

Hugging my knees, toes
curled over the edge
Watching the sun dance
on the sea
Staring out at the never
ending ocean
Stretching out as far as the
eye can see and further
still
Forever.

With each salty, wispy
breath
With every wave that
crashed and lapped and
sprayed that luscious sea
spray
With the salty sea breeze
Came fresh thoughts and a

new beginning

A calm new start

Staring out at the raging

sea.

I Swear

If you cut me open, I
swear,
The sea would pour out.
My breath passes my lips
As salty whispers of the
ocean
And my eyes roll out the
waves
Meant to crash against the
shore.

Long Road Home

Pounding on the
pavement.
Heavy steps,
Cutting into my bare,
Broken soles.
Each step
Encrusted in brittle stones.
But this is my path.
My shoeless feet will carry
me home,
Through the rough
And unknown roads.
Until the dust
Becomes a part of me,
And my blood
Seeps into the stone.

The Map of Your Skin

Take the curves
And grooves
And scars on your skin.
Fill them in
With ink
And let them
Be your map.
They show
Where you have been
And where
You long to go.

You'll Find Happiness in the Morning

"Don't worry about it,
everything will be better
in the morning," he smiles
to her.
"But how do you know?"
she replies with her eyes
full of wonderment.
It was such a simple
question
Yet it held the weight of
the world
Within its breath.
Through the sigh of a man
Who has seen such
questions left unanswered
before,
He softly murmurs,
"Because my darling,

When you sleep,
The stars watch over you
in wonder
And your dreams drift
with you
To everything that makes
you happy.
If you close your eyes tight
You can go wherever you
want
But when you dream
You feel it in your bones.
It leads you to happiness
It may take all your time
dreaming
But you'll make it there.
And when you wake up
You realise
You were already there to
start with.
All you needed

Was to open your eyes

again.

So sleep now sweetheart,

And I'll see you when you

get back."

Habits

Half of my life is a living
habit.
I drink tea in the
mornings and I miss you,
Purely out of habit.
Sometimes I still talk to
you
Like you're here,
Even though you're long
gone,
Because I'm in the habit of
pretending
You're still around.
I wear eyeliner on the
waterline
And put myself down
Because that's what I'm
used to.

And there's this one
person
Who I fall in and out of
habit with;
When we meet we fall into
each other's existence
As if we see each other
every day
And our lips collide.
But only out of habit.
That feeling too has long
gone.
But I'd still kiss him
And I'll always talk to you,
In awe of the stars.
Habitude.
And sometimes I want to
live outside of habits,
So I don't wear the
bracelets I wear every day

And I'll see you and keep
my distance
And I'll talk to the people
Who are still here with
me,
Instead of those I've lost
And I won't long for the
beach
But for the woods instead.
But I usually go back to
my old ways
Where I miss you again.
Back to those self-
ingrained habits.

The Zoo

Let's go to the zoo
Enjoy simple things again
Like we did as children.
Let's go for a ride
Roam everywhere
And nowhere
Just for the joy of being.
Let's go for a walk
Through the fields
Climb trees and scuff our
knees
Swing legs over the edge.
Let's dive into the sea
No fear
Brace the cool waves
Feel life again.
This summer,
Let's go to the zoo.

Leave

I bought a ticket.
Packed my bags
And bought a ticket.
One way.
Because I'm not coming
back.
I don't care if you're not in
I'll sit on the doorstep
And wait
While the cold creeps
round me
I'll wait.
Until you're home
To let me in
Greet me with a hug
And let me in.
Into the warmth.
I'm not going back.

The Anger of the Storm

The sky suddenly filled
with light
Forked across the Earth
"One Mississippi, Two
Mississippi, Three
Mississippi…"
A grumble is heard, far
away
The God's are not happy
And no one knows why
But there's a threatening
sound
From the anger of the sky

Another flash terrorises
the clouds
As they pour down with
fear
"One Mississippi, Two
Mississippi…"
Closer and louder the sky
roars down
Threatening the living far

below
The people quiver; afraid
it's their turn
That one false move would
anger the sky near
As a million sorrys are
whispered in fear

Light fills the clouds once
more
"One Mississippi…"
It's overhead now
The anger of the storm
Bearing down on us
And wondering what
we're worth

A cold wind whips away
at the clouds
And pushes the lightening
away
*"One Mississippi, Two
Mississippi…"*
It's passing over us now

And a thousand thanks are
sent to the wind
That blew away the storm.

A Broken Plate For A Broken Home

It cracks in two under the
sheer force of anger
Dividing what it holds into
separate islands
Parting unevenly
A jagged split.
Leaving baited breath and
shockwaves of rage
Pushing the islands
further apart
Smashed and fragile...
Try and fix it with glue
like the rest of this place
Even the strongest still
shows the cracks...
Of the broken plate
Sitting in the broken
cupboard,

Hanging on the hinges of
a broken home.

I'm Trying Not To Care Anymore

You raised hellish dust
with hurtful words
Aggravating the land and
scaring scavenging birds
Who pick at the dead
crops growing fruitlessly
from dry soil
Now from dizzy heights
they watch you bubble
and boil
As you spill insults onto
the earths cracked skin
Watch it soak it all up and
take it all in
The dusts still rise to a
hellish level
Taking a ride with demons
and the devil
So let the dusts settle in

lonely lands
With the fugitive heat and
sardonic sands
Things will not be how
they were before
For I care not about you
anymore.

There's A Storm Inside My Mind

The storm clouds rage
And march onwards
While a dark mist
descends
Pushing forwards
constantly.
The battering winds
And relentless downpour
Causes the mist to lower
Chills sweep the land.
A break in the sky
Catches the last glimpse of
sun
Before it is engulfed
In the rain.
Bright lights sear through
the thick layer of fog

Wipers monotonously
moving
Left, right, left, right, left
Racing to shelter
Raincoats pulled tight
As the clap of thunder
Echoes the click of the
door.
Raindrops lace my
window
And I'm caught in the
storm
Once more.

The Outsider

Sprawled out
Legs hanging over the
edge of the chair
Toes tapping to the music
But not quite on time
Humming along
To the wrong tune
Glass in hand
And a smile which doesn't
quite meet her eyes.

Mortal Angel

Half fledged wings
protrude from the hollow
curve of my back
Too angular
Pushed back.
Corners pointed as limbs
are folded in sharp angles
Still too angular
Arms wrapped round
Fingers instead of feathers
As only the blades are a
reminder
I cut off my wings for a
mortal soul
Now only mortal sins
remain.

Dead Man's Time

Sitting on the hill with
your back against the
wind as it chills through
you.
Staring out at the crashing
waves like you did before.
When you were whole
and the wind battered
your body
And ruffled your hair.
Now you're stuck in limbo
to wander the streets
Endlessly and alone.
Time means nothing;
Just endless eternity
stretching forever ahead
of you.
But you have no one to
share it with,
Nothing to fill it with

And you wonder to

yourself,

How does a dead man kill

time?

Mr Wolf

"What's the time Mr
Wolf?"
The children used to sing
But time went by with
temptation tied
And Mr Wolf never said a
thing.

"Maybe he's a vegetarian,"
they cried
"Or perhaps he just
doesn't care"
Yet they knew deep down
something was wrong
From the changes in the
air.

Now his hair has grown
thin and he often thinks

About the children he
would normally engulf
Who to such a dangerous
beast they fondly sing
“What’s the matter Mr
Wolf?”

Like Father, Like Daughter

Leading the way
With a glass in his hand
Teaching me the wisdom
Of this sordid land.
Like father, like daughter
The sorrowful delve
I've been practically an
alcoholic
Since the age of twelve.

Nosocomephobia

Nails biting at the palms of
my hands
Where they've balled up in
fear.
And I don’t care about the
piercing pain
Because it takes my mind
off the lump in my throat
And the wires protruding
from your pale skin.
The raw red lines
scorching my own skin
Stop me thinking about
how fragile you sound,
Voice like aged paper
That's been moth-eaten
and torn.
Yet I still can't talk
For the lump in my throat
And the worrisome tears

Stinging at my eyes.
I know it's just my own
fear
And you'll be perfectly
fine,
But I find it creepily ironic
That my stomach turns
And skin crawls
In the place supposed to
make you feel better.

The Signature of the Rose

It tears
Straight across
My skin.
Leaving Morse Code
Dashes
Etched in the shape
Of a scar.
And the smallest
Thorn
Protrudes from the edge.
The signature
Of the rose.

The Pain That No One Knows

Raw from the memories
she slides down against
the wall.
Curling her knees up to
her chest
And wrapping her arms
protectively around
herself,
As if to pull herself
together again.
But it's been left too long
On its own for it to heal.
The gaping hole in her
chest.
Ragged from memory.
Something missing but
nothing to fill it with.

The emptiness makes her
shudder
As a harsh wind of truth
Batters the sides of her
wounded body.
Soft whimpers escape her
quivering lips.
Fresh tears burn trails in
her cheeks
As they run furiously
down,
Splashing painfully onto
her broken body.
Resting her head on her
knees she closes her eyes
And allows the final
teardrops to sting her eyes
And fall plumply on her
sodden knee.
Everything she could
remember,

All the happiness she had
felt,
Slowly ebbed away from
her being.
Losing the light of life
As it slowly fades into
nothing.
Reduced to nothing,
Sat perfectly still,
Everything that might be
hurt drawing in.
Until it was just her.
An empty shell.
Alone.
Feeling empty and cold.
Curled against the wall.
Just wishing for that last
piece.
For the pain to melt away.

The simplicity of expression

You look at me in that
simple way.
One expression;
One emotion.
But I can't work it out
Can't put my finger on it.
He changes face
Shadows and furrows his
brow
Tries to put his finger on
my own expression.
I know that it's simple too
Yet in a different way;
Blank.
Maybe that's why I don't
understand him
I don't understand myself.
Trying to search for a soul
Or break down barriers
with a kiss.
It hasn't worked yet.

I'm sorry.
It's better this way
For me at least
So don't waste your
emotions
On heartless memories.

Innamorato

Innamorato.
The word lies on my
tongue as you lay next to
me.
Sweet and desired;
Silent on my lips
Yet it burns like a fire in
my body.
Lustful and beautiful
You sleep next to me,
My eyes wandering over
you.
Innamorato,
Dormendo, coricasti.
Breathing in your sweet
scent
And breaking the urge
To plant soft kisses on
your slightly parted lips.

The fire burns in my soul
And I whisper the word
breathlessly into your ear.
Handing you my heart
And my burning soul
As I whisper that word...
Innamorato...
Lover...

Old Habits Die Hard

We make new promises
To ourselves and everyone
else
But the truth still lies
In that fleeting glance
I can see it in your eyes
It glimmers in your soul
And I want to reach out
To hold it
Take a piece for my own.
Slip back to the old ways,
They always seem better at
the time
So why not?
I know the harm,
But I'll be careful this time
Less involved
Yet not entirely detached.
You bring me my senses
And take them away too
One word

And I'm yours
In a breath or less.
That look takes me back.
Meet me there?

Stupidity With You

How could I be so stupid?
I lost myself; tangled in
emotions.
Why do I let you run riot
with my mind?
You know what to say and
I hate it
Yet I love it and I never
stop it…
Maybe it’s my fault.
Maybe I'm the one to
blame
Either way it can't go on.
It feels right, it feels wrong
I feel nothing at all
But that burning desire,
and you're calling my
name
In that way that you do
The way I can't resist.

Restrain me and my
feelings
They don't belong with
you.
Or maybe they do and
you're the one who's
wrong...
But that's just it; that
word, it sums it up.
It's wrong.

To Change What We Have Done

No more games.
Just me and you
And shared vulnerability
As I stand before you
Emotionally bare.
Laying everything I have
In front of me
And you do the same.
Dismantling your armour.
I've never seen you so
honest
Stripped of your defences.
So now what?
What happens now?
With us?
Our friendship has
changed

Let's go back to what we
were.
I've lost my closest friend.
You can't even face me
Can't be around me
For a while.
Now fragile bones rattle in
the wind
And tears of realisation
Sting behind my eyes
As we face what we have
done.

Shadows Will Remind Me

There are smooth dark
shadows lying beneath my
eyes,
And I'm trying to work out
If they are the reminder of
you
I asked for at
3:19 this morning.
When I was afraid I was
forgetting
How you towered above
me
And made me banana and
chocolate spread
sandwiches
And if your teeth were
straight or crooked.
And you had gone before I
could wish you happy
birthday

But I sent you a card
anyway
In case by some luck
The postman would
deliver it
3.6 days earlier.
But there were too many
clouds in the sky that
night, so I couldn't see
enough stars
To make a wish that big.
If I could
Now I'd ask them for one
more day
When you were strong
enough
For me to stand on your
toes
And you could see
How big and bad I've
grown

For my bones are rotting
away with yours.
And I'd want you to watch
me leave once more
So I don't have to keep
looking back
Waiting for you to be
there.

All The Words In The World, Can't Sum Up How I Feel

Sometimes
I feel like I've used all my
words up
Exhausted all the ones I
know
And searched for new
ones every step of the way.

Yet I don't think I've found
a way to describe how I
feel
Through all the words
The phrases
The sayings, quotes, lyrics
I cannot find ones
To sum up
How I feel about
everything

And how I feel about

myself.

Love Is Far From Simple, Darling

They say that love is just a
simple thing.
And I don't know who
they are,
But it's not.
It's really not.
Love is the hardest thing
You will ever have to
come to terms with.
And how do you
understand it?
Like do I love you,
Of course I do,
But am I in love with you?
I don't know.
Like I know that you love
me,

But you're not *in love with me.*
You love me like summer nights
And your goldfish you had as a child
And old memories
And video games
And I love you just the same,
Except that I didn't have a goldfish
When I was younger and
I've never been good at video games.
And I don't know how to deal
With knowing that you love me
But that you don't,

And not knowing if I love
you
Or if I don't,
But maybe I should find
Someone else to write
about.

61.9 Reasons

I am 75 daisies
Chained together for luck
And early morning's
thoughts.
When I'm nervous
I think of you
And broken fairy tales
And how many fish there
are in the sea.
And there are 61.9 reasons
Why you shouldn't love
me
And 3600 seconds
When I will forget the
world
To love you back.
But my eyes are not pretty
like others'
So I struggle to see the
pretty things in the world.

I hope someday,
Someone will make you
happy
But that you can still see
the broken pieces
Of me in her eyes.
I hope I can find
somewhere to belong.

I have counted 41796
stars,
And named them all after
you.

www.ingramcontent.com/pod-product-compliance
Ingram Content Group UK Ltd.
Pitfield, Milton Keynes, MK11 3LW, UK
UKHW020232250726
13967UKWH00001B/328

9 781471 792366